Critical Acclaim for *Got, Not Got*

Runner-up, Best Football Book, British Sports Book Awards 2012
Got, Not Got: The A-Z of Lost Football Culture, Treasures & Pleasures

"A veritable Dundee cake of a book."
Danny Kelly, talkSport

"Recalling a more innocent time before Sky Sports and millionaire players, *Got, Not Got* is like a long soak in a warm bath of football nostalgia: an A-Z of memorabilia, ephemera and ill-advised haircuts."
In Demand, *Mail on Sunday Live* magazine

"The real magic is the collection and display of the illustrative material of stickers, badges, programme covers, Subbuteo figures and other ephemera. It is astonishingly thorough, well-presented, inspired and indeed had me going, 'yes, got, got, not got, forgot, never seen'."
When Saturday Comes

"A cracking book which whisks you back to a different footballing era."
Brian Reade, Mirror Football

"This memorabilia fest is a delightful reminder of what's gone from the game: 'magic sponges', Subbuteo and, er, magazines for shinpads. Such innocent times, eh?"
FourFourTwo

"The book's great fun. It's an essential if you grew up watching football in the 60s, 70s or 80s. It's a kind of football fan's catnip. Nobody can quite walk past it. They start looking at it and then realise they've got something else they should be doing 10 or 15 minutes later."
Paul Hawksbee, talkSport.

"The best book about football written in the last 20 years."
Bill Borrows, *Esquire*

"A body of work that transcends being 'just a book' by a considerable distance."
In Bed With Maradona blog

"Obviously, everybody over the age of 40 is going to absolutely love this.
There's something for every fan of every club."
Andy Jacobs, talkSport

"Browsable for hours, even days, preferably with your favourite records from the 1970s in the background, this is the Christmas present that every football fan of a certain age yearns to peruse while their neglected partner's busy basting the turkey and getting quietly pickled on cooking sherry… Sit back and be blissfully reminded of adverts, food products, players, toys, kits, magazines, stickers and trends you'd long since confined to your mental attic."
Ian Plenderleith, Stay-at-Home Indie Pop blog

"I've had this for a month but haven't got round to reviewing it because it keeps disappearing.
It's the sign of a good book that people repeatedly pick it up and walk away with it.
A hardback collection of vintage football memorabilia that you need in your life…
It's like finding your old football stickers."
James Brown, SabotageTimes.com

"No. 339: The book *Got, Not Got*."
500 Reasons To Love Football blog

"Wallow in the days of your youth until your heart is content, as the days when you were a football mad youngster come flooding back. If someone wants to buy you a Christmas present, then ask for this. You will not be disappointed."
United Review Collectors Club Newsletter

"It is a work of genius, I cannot state this too highly. The most brilliant book I've opened in a long, long time."
Monica Winfield, BBC Radio Leicester

"Those were indeed the days"
Those Were The Days: The Independent Ipswich Town website.

"An excellent and unusual new football book."
Fly Me To The Moon, Middlesboro fanzine

"The must-have Christmas book"
Derby County Football Card Collection

"*Got, Not Got* is an affectionate and humorous celebration of football's pre-sanitised era: when players clutched their cuffs, Derby County won the league and dads did the pools. A timely, and welcome, exercise in nostalgia."
ShortList

"I can guarantee that virtually anybody who flicks open this magnificent book will immediately want to have it. Whatever you have loved about our game, it will almost certainly be buried within this lavish trove of treasure."
Winger: The Review of British Football

"The perfect stocking filler for Christmas."
Mike Lawrence, BBC Radio London

"It's a beauty. An absolute must-have for all you nostalgia junkies out there. Wonderful articles and evocative images and above all lots of fun, *Got, Not Got* has it all. Treat yourself or your football-mad relatives to one of the best football books around."
footysphere.com

"It's a real table thumper with some weight to it, great pictures and some terrific writing. Bathe in a sea of nostalgia and rail against the fact that these things aren't there anymore."
Nick Godwin, BBC Radio London

"A fantastic book, there's just so much in it. You really should get it."
Steve Anglesey, Mirror Football podcast

"It focuses on the 1960s, 70s and 80s, and anyone who had anything to do with English football during this period will instantly relate to just about every page. I'm sure that you will both laugh and cry as the memories come flooding back."
Nigel Mercer, Football Card Webspace

Pitch Publishing Ltd
A2 Yeoman Gate
Yeoman Way
Durrington
BN13 3QZ

Email: info@pitchpublishing.co.uk
Web: www.pitchpublishing.co.uk

First published by Pitch Publishing 2013
Text © 2013 Derek Hammond and Gary Silke

Derek Hammond and Gary Silke have asserted their rights in accordance with the Copyright, Designs and Patents Act 1988 to be identified as the authors of this work.

All rights reserved. No part of this publication may be reproduced, stored in a retrieval system, or transmitted in any form or by any means, electronic, mechanical, photocopying, recording or otherwise, without the prior permission in writing of the publisher and the copyright owners, or as expressly permitted by law, or under terms agreed with the appropriate reprographics rights organization. Enquiries concerning reproduction outside the terms stated here should be sent to the publishers at the UK address printed on this page.

The publisher makes no representation, express or implied, with regard to the accuracy of the information contained in this book and cannot accept any legal responsibility for any errors or omissions that may be made.

A CIP catalogue record for this book is available from the British Library.

13-digit ISBN: 9781909178748
Design and typesetting by Olner Pro Sport Media.
Printed in the UK by CPI Group (UK), Croydon CR0 4YY

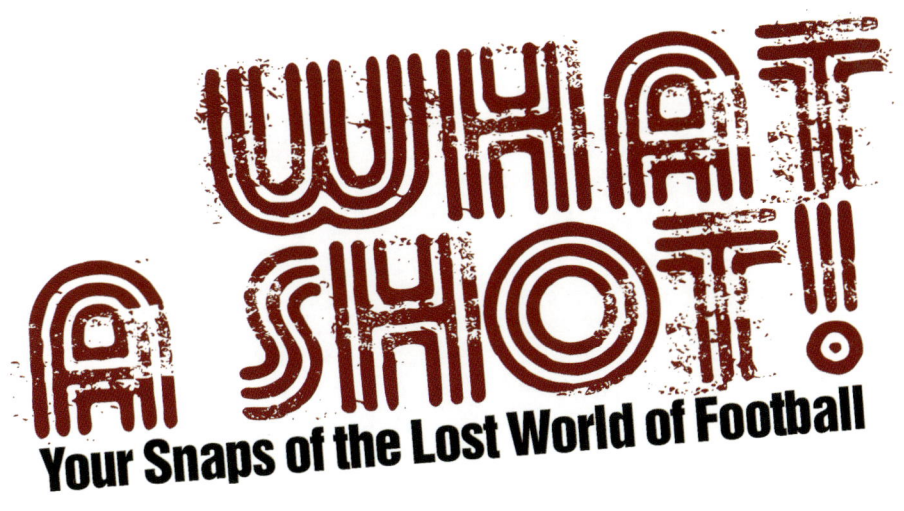

Your Snaps of the Lost World of Football

**Gary Silke &
Derek Hammond**

Thanks to those of you who sent us your photos of the lost world of football, which we've added to our own to produce this collection.

We'll have to ask readers to forgive the occasional lack of focus, the over-exposure, the murkiness, the big heads in the way – the pictures were largely taken with happy snappy cameras like this (in fact some of them were actually taken with this camera) with nothing but a single button to press.

Before the giddy days of digital photography, when you can fire off two-dozen shots and bin all but the best one, you had to wait a couple of days until Boots had processed your film, then sit on the bench outside on the High Street and open the envelope… and usually experience a slight twinge of disappointment. They'd always looked so much better through the viewfinder.

But you can't stick a quality control sticker on life, and now we've come to love their shortcomings – and, anyway, we couldn't go and retake them even if we wanted to.

The moment has long passed, and many of the places recorded here are now changed beyond recognition, or lost forever.

We hope you enjoy the pictures and any shared memories they might stir up.

Gary Silke and Derek Hammond

Caged Throstle: West Brom's emblem lost amid ugly '80s metalwork.

Get the floodlights on!:
A drab day at The Hawthorns.

Old Trafford – Theatre of Dreams:
Or nightmares if you're in the away end.

Lost, but not forgotten: Archibald Leitch's grand old Trinity Road Stand, 1922-2000. And a splendid woolly hat.

Losing sight of your goal:
Fenced in at The Dell.

Leicester defend a corner at Southampton in 1986. Note the angled standing area behind the seats in the lower tier of the East Stand.

Standing room only: a chilly afternoon at Vicarage Road.

Shallow terracing in Watford's Rookery afforded a great view of the backs of heads.

The Anfield Experience:
Guy Keeley's photos of
Liverpool v Bristol City, October 1979.

Blurred, big heads, fences and bags of atmosphere.

Julian Simpson's photo diary of a season – Brighton on Tour, 1988-89; clockwise:

Top left: The East Stand and Shed End at Chelsea, and some classic illuminated backs of heads.

Top centre: On the tilt at Sunderland's Roker Park.

Top right and middle left: The condemned Riverside Stand being dismantled at Blackburn. That's a lot of red for a team that plays in blue and white.

Middle centre: The West Stand at Stamford Bridge.

Bottom left: Watching the action at Elland Road through a spiked fence, on the same day as the Hillsborough Disaster.

Bottom right: A new Main Stand has risen from the ashes at Valley Parade, but a fresh football disaster is about to strike.

Brighton on Tour, 1988-89; Part Two, clockwise:

Top left: The recently condemned and demolished Fratton End leaves a yawning gap.

Top centre: An uphill task at the County Ground, where the upper tier of the Shrivenham Stand is out of commission.

Top right: The distinctive white wall that surrounded Vicarage Road doesn't prevent a quick peek at the action.

Middle centre: Lethal tinsel at Boothferry Park.

Middle right: The Brewery Stand at Barnsley carries an appropriate roof ad.

Bottom left: A view of the 'aquarium on stilts' North Stand from Pen One of the Spion Kop, Filbert Street.

Bottom centre: Playing on the lino at Boundary Park.

Bottom right: A restricted view from the Bramall Lane end at Sheffield United.

Robert Nichols, editor of Boro's *Fly Me To The Moon* fanzine, pays a last visit to the Holgate End on the open weekend in 1997 when Ayresome Park was closed down, soon to be demolished. Robert bought some toilet signs as keepsakes, and they're now installed in his new home — which stands on the site of the old Boys' End.

Prenton Park, after Tranmere Rovers had beaten Exeter in the final game of 1986-87 to avoid becoming the first team to be automatically relegated out of the Football League. "It's probably a good job the photo is blurred," reckons Steve McKeown.

Nick Richards snaps a full house at Carrow Road for the visit of Man United... and some very '80s hair.

Oakridge FC of Stafford, back in the 1967-68 season. "My primary school team," says Deryck Wilson. "I am far right – one sock up, one down."

Into the Valley: Plenty of room on Charlton's enormous East Bank.

How Green Was My Valley: Steve McKeown at Charlton during the wilderness years.

The East Bank in even further reduced circumstances later during Charlton's exile.

Parent & Child £5: Quite a bargain at Partick Thistle's old turnstiles.

The art deco main gates are all that remain of the sorely missed Feethams, Darlington.

Alan Hansen gets to meet Liverpool's Simon Kidd.

Right: Julian Joachim gets to meet Andy Sibson's Mum.

Below left: Chris Bignell and Peter 'the Cat' Bonetti.

Below right: "11 years old at a Pontins holiday camp in Paignton, Devon, circa 1982. I'm actually (and always have been) a West Ham supporter but the sports shop in my home town of Barking didn't have the similarly pinstriped Norwich City kit that I really wanted, so I chose the Liverpool kit as my second best option. The other thing is that I'm standing next to the former world professional snooker champion, Ray Reardon. This was not a regular occurrence in my childhood years; he just happened to be at the holiday camp doing a demonstration of trick shots and the like for the assembled punters." Chris Oakley.

Top left: Steve Bull gets to meet Marie Elwell.

Top right: Ian Rands and his old mukka Keith Edwards.

Below: "Preston's St Maria Goretti Cubs in 1975/76. We won the League and Cup, and were unbeaten all season. We got both trophies presented to us by Preston North End's players of the time; striker Mike Elwiss and goalkeeper Roy Tunks. Happy times, great kits." Bill Routledge

Top: Dean Benfield blends seamlessly into this 1981-82 Leicester City team group.

Left: "Me and Frankie Wortho taken minutes after Birmingham had just gubbed us 6-2 on the frozen pitch in December 1976. I can remember the conversation word-for-word:
Frank: 'Ooh, smokey bacon - my favourite!'
Me: 'They're plain.'"
Andy Pateman

Right: Chelsea fan John Appleton meets West Ham and England legend Bobby Moore (whose middle name was actually Chelsea).

The Hair Bear Bunch: Opening day of the 1980-81 season at Carrow Road.

Just when you think you've taken a half-decent photo of Justin Fashanu & Co. bashing Stoke 5-1... it turns out there's a bloody hair in the gate.

Andy Starmore captures the essence of late 1970s Elland Road.

All eyes on me: Liverpool arrive at Elland Road.

Leeds v Liverpool 1979, when you still had a view down Elland Road from the West Stand.

In the dark: You'll never guess where this is...

Not on my Manor: Oxford's London Road end. Pitch invasion not an option.

The Manor: Lots of stands to chose from. Approximately nine, at last count.

Panorama-mania! A gloomy day at Eastville, viewed over the greyhound track...

Parkaeology: The last vestiges of Man City's Maine Road home — a sky-blue drainpipe and a gate to nowhere under the razor wire.

Imps v Gills at Sincil Bank, in January 1982. "Quite what possessed me to take a camera along on such a forlorn day, I've no idea," says Ian Plenderleith. "There's some good 1980s hairstyles and anoraks. I'm guessing they're Queen fans – punk still hadn't reached Lincolnshire. The Imps keeper is David Felgate, who was almost a Welsh international."

Going Bananas: Manchester City's famous Boxing Day trip to Stoke in 1988. "City took 12,000 that day and the players came out on the pitch carrying bananas," remembers John Ashton. "City were 1-0 up at half time, then, during the break, someone in the hardest section of the home crowd stuck a stray banana on the barbed-wire fence and burst it. Stoke then came out and scored three quick goals and we were sunk."

City did get promoted out of Division Two in that great banana season of 1988-89. Here's Frankenstein and mates at Selhurst Park, where City drew 0-0. Banana shots dedicated to the memory of the man who took them, Graham Stirling (inset).

All change at Crewe: Cinder banking and tiny stands at Gresty Road, soon to be replaced. Sadly, they ditched the novel 'third goal' experiment as well, after going down 6-5-1 to Doncaster in the Cup.

Tales from the Riverbank:
The Trent End, Nottingham Forest in 1987.

Old Trafford, 1987:
Back in the days when it held a mere 58,000.

Heads up: A view of the Stretford End.

Just not cricket: Brutal architecture at Bramall Lane, where once stood the wicket.

They don't build streets like this anymore. Or vans.

Sheffield Steel: A view of the John Street Stand at Bramall Lane.

Two views of the giant Holte End at Villa Park, which held 22,000. And an absolutely planetary head.

Holy Trinity: One of football's cathedrals in 1986.
Sadly no longer with us.

Leicester fans sample the pies at Elland Road in 1987.
Nom, nom, nom.

Made from Girders:
Looking up at Aldershot and Orient.

Probably should have used the flash: Norwich and Leicester grope about at Carrow Road in 1986.

View of the Boundary: Oldham's windswept home is the third highest league ground in England. There aren't many Portakabins hovering this far off the ground, either.

Nocturnal Owls: The flash lights up a head, and a Hillsborough fence that was to become tragically infamous three years later.

Withdean and I: Brighton's 'temporary' home for twelve years.

The back end of Workington:
That's a proper shade of red, is that.

Borough Park, Workington. Remarkably similar to the football grounds we used to draw.

One day, all this will be chalets: The Bobbers Stand at Kenilworth Road, Luton two years after Millwall fans attempted to demolish it in 1985.

Plastic pitch, fences and a small marketing-related castle at Luton: It can only be the '80s.

Derby days: The Baseball Ground, complete with brass band and ram out on the mudbath, in its pomp at the end of the '60s.

... and in its final days, recorded by Andy Ellis.

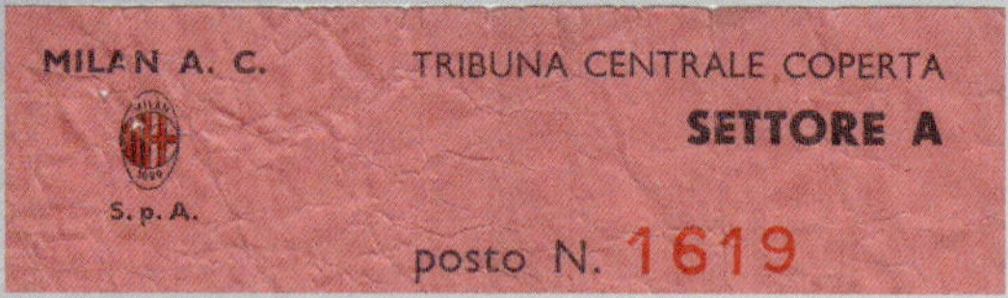
MILAN A. C.
S.p.A.
TRIBUNA CENTRALE COPERTA
SETTORE A
posto N. 1619

COMMANDOS TIGRE

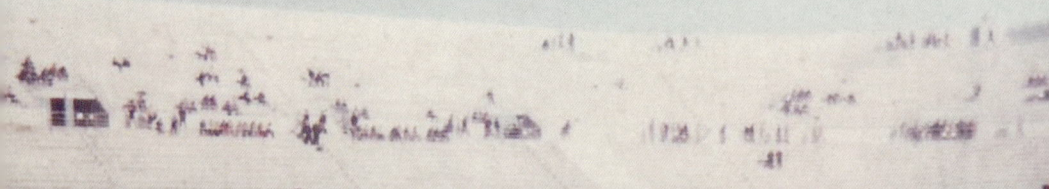

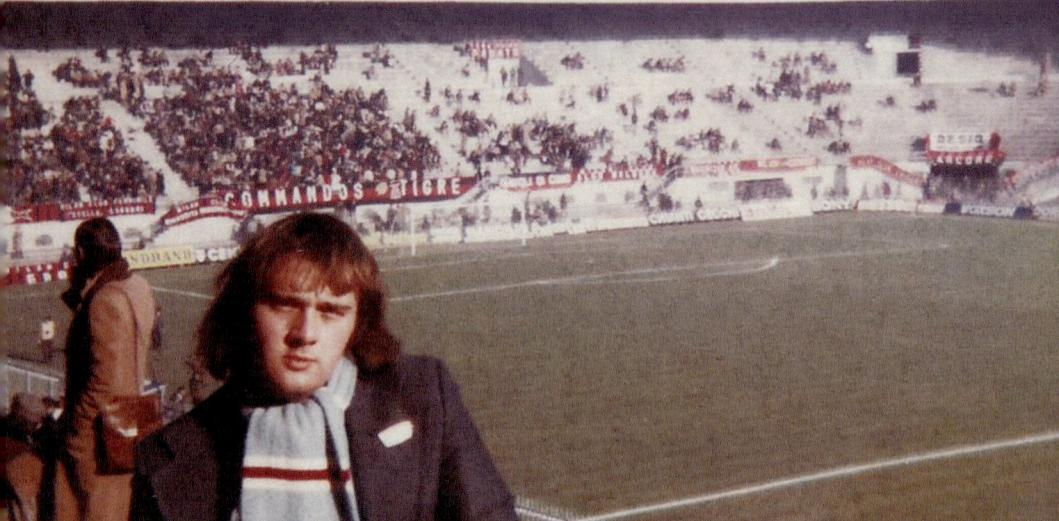

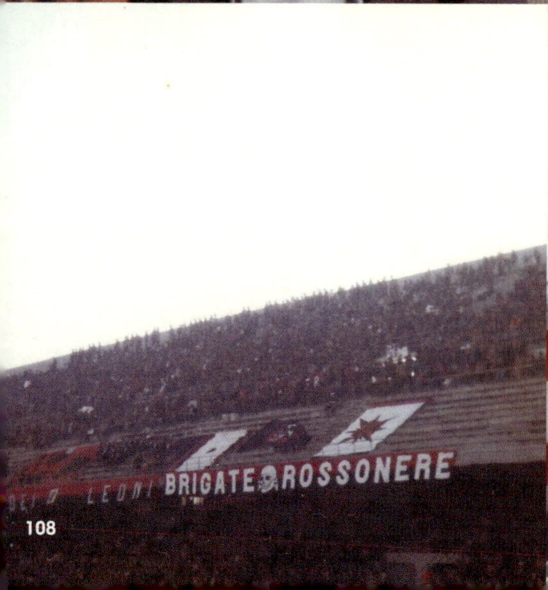
BRIGATE ROSSONERE

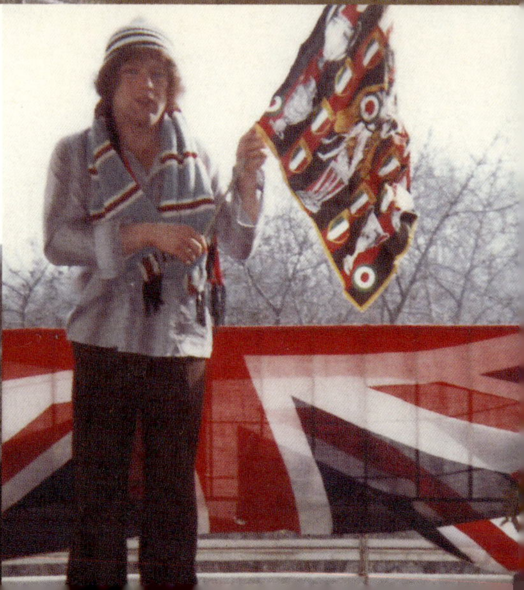

AC Milan v Man City, UEFA Cup Third Round first leg, November 1978: Here's Anthony Heywood and his mate Brian on the balcony at their hotel, as well as shots of Tony, the oppo fans and match action at the ground.

"The match was called off due to fog and played the following afternoon," he recalls. "But unfortunately, due to flights, we could only stay and see the first half!"

Still, at least they got to watch the second half on TV on the coach. Paul Power put City two up before Milan clawed back to a 2-2 draw.

City won the second leg 3-0 at Maine Road.

Rotting Hull: Boothferry's giant floodlights persist.

Uphill task: Chris Donald's Kodacolor trannie of Newcastle v Spurs in 1974.

On the next spread, there's more from Chris at St. James', at a big game against Blackpool Reserves. Look out for the jolly seaside ice-cream stall on the end of the empty, brutal terrace, presumably the only away fan.

David Jameson captures Mirandinha's grand entrance in a very, very white jacket in 1987.

Leicester clinch the Second Division title at Orient in May 1980, and celebrating fans snap the crossbar.
These photos were found on a rubbish tip along with a final demand phone bill from Post Office Telecommunications addressed to City centre-half Geoff Scott (who appears in the inset photo).

A TV tower at Bognor Regis Town, for which the word 'rickety' might have been invented. Luckily, there's not much call for TV cameras at Bognor.

And a game at Tranmere from April 1973. The floodlight to the left is at Chesterfield's old Saltergate home, now flattened.

Something in Reserve: George Chilvers' snaps of Everton v Manchester City stiffs at Goodison.

The fairly grandstand at Petersfield Town.

The End: Rust and crumbling terraces at Benburb. "The Scottish Juniors apparently broke away from the Scottish FA in 1931," says Andy Ormerod. "I guess that's when they ditched their rules on ground grading and safety. They used to get crowds of up to 10,000 here in the old days – there were 50 last Wednesday."

The Ghost Ground: Only trees now stand on the terraces at Third Lanark's Cathkin Park. It's only 10 minutes' walk from Hampden – definitely worth a visit if you're in Glasgow.

Filbert Street's Spion Kop and Double Decker.
Inset: Queuing to get into the Kop, in the days when you were thoroughly searched before reaching the turnstiles.

The classical turnstile block on Filbert Street. Local rumour has it, it was rescued during demolition and resides somewhere in a builder's yard. We hope so.

"The famous Wakeman End wooden scoreboard meant a lot to me," says Mike Schorah. "As a kid I stood underneath it, especially on wet days when it afforded the only cover on the Wakeman Terrace." Here, you can see it as it was in 1986, and then on the disastrous day it was needlessly demolished in May 1996.

Gay Meadow: "It was decrepit, but home," admits Mike.

The Meadow's Station Road turnstile, dating back to 1885, came from the old Crystal Palace ground that staged Cup Finals around the turn of the 20th century.

Telegraph Sport: Aldershot rely on the old ways.

Mobile sales:
Completely sold out at Southport.

Leeds visit Dean Court, Bournemouth in 1988.

Some tickets still available:
From Hull City's box office.

142

The Authors

Gary Silke and Derek Hammond are also the authors of *The Lost World of Football* (Pitch, 2013), *Got, Not Got: The Lost World of Manchester United, Leeds United* and *West Ham United* (all Pitch, 2013) and *Got, Not Got: The A-Z of Lost Football Culture, Treasures & Pleasures* (Pitch, 2011).

Roll the Credits
in order of appearance...

Gary Silke: 4, 6, 8, 10, 12, 14, 15, 16, 17, 18, 20, 66, 67, 68, 69, 70, 71, 72, 73, 74, 76, 77, 78, 80, 81, 82, 84, 88, 92, 100, 102, 103, 128, 129, 130.
Guy Keeley: 22, 23, 24, 25, 44, 46, 54, 56, 58, 59.
Julian Simpson: 26, 27, 28, 29.
Robert Nichols: 30 (top).
Steve McKeown: 30 (bottom), 36 (top).
Nick Richards: 31.
Deryck Wilson: 32.
Unknown photographer: 34, 35.
Allan Norris: 36 (bottom).
Andy Ormerod: 37 (top), 86, 118, 122, 124, 126.
Mike Schorah: 37 (bottom), 87, 90, 94, 96, 98, 110, 120 (left), 132, 133, 134, 136, 137, 138, 139, 142.
Simon Kidd: 38.
Andy Sibson: 40 (top).
Chris Bignell: 40 (bottom left).
Chris Oakley: 40 (bottom right).
Marie Elwell: 41 (top left).
Ian Rands: 41 (top right).
Bill Routledge: 41 (bottom).
Andy Pateman: 42.
Dean Benfield: 43 (top).
John Appleton: 43 (bottom).
Andy Starmore: 48, 49, 50, 52, 140.
Ian Plenderleith: 60 (top).
David Mayor: 60 (bottom).
Graham Stirling/John Ashton: 62, 64.
Andy McConachie: 104.
Andy Ellis: 106, 107.
Anthony Heywood and Brian: 108, 109.
Chris Donald: 112, 114 (top), 115 (top), back cover.
David Jameson: 114 (bottom), 115 (bottom).
Rubbish tip photos: 116.
George Chilvers: 120 (top and bottom), 121.
Gavin Hadland: back cover.

More Critical Acclaim for *Got, Not Got*

"This exquisite book is a homage to the game of 40 years ago – not just the mudheaps and the mavericks but a celebration of its wider culture [which] rises above lazy, modern-life-is-rubbish nostalgia… The design is so sumptuous and the stories so well chosen and written that it's hard to resist the authors' conclusion that much – call it charm, character or even romance – has been lost in the rush for cash. Regardless of whether it really was a golden age, this is a golden volume, as much a social history as a sports book. If you've not got *Got, Not Got*, you've got to get it."
Backpass

"I can guarantee that virtually anybody who flicks open this magnificent book will immediately want to have it."
The Football Trader

"For further reminders of the long-lost game of the 1960s, '70s and '80s, the illuminating new book *Got, Not Got* does a very fine job."
Sport magazine

"If, like myself, you are an unashamed nostalgia junkie, this book is for you. It's more than just a book on football collectables, including memories and experiences from the golden age – a time before the FA Premiership and TV money took us through a pound-sign portal and into a parallel, but much less likeable, universe. Some of my favourite experiences/memories are included – I found myself saying either 'did it' or 'remember it' – and there's a heck of a lot to choose from."
Programme Monthly

"A huge success and an epic tome for lovers of football nostalgia everywhere."
The Football Attic blog

"It's an absolute beauty."
Adrian Goldberg, BBC Radio WM.

"An absolute gem of a book – part brilliantly written lament for an earlier age, part opportunity to reminisce about a time when you hankered after a Garden Goal ('Every Boy's Dream!')… Football's relentless commercialisation comes, naturally enough, at a cost. It's brought us everything from the Stalinist-style obliteration of the game's pre-1992 history to the modern player, kissing the badge, logo and sponsor's name after scoring. A purer, less cynical era is depicted throughout *Got, Not Got*. Buy it – you will not be disappointed."
SportsBookoftheMonth.com

"The best dose of retro football nostalgia ever. I can't put it down!"
footballcardsuk.com

"It's a beautiful book – a smorgasbord!"
John Keith, City Talk FM, Liverpool

"An exhaustively researched collection of football programmes, stickers, badges and memorabilia, a coffee table book you can dip in and out of at any time. Some of the advertisements from old programmes are classics – 'Bovril – hot favourite for the cup!' Or culinary advice to players: 'Full English – eat up your fried bread now, it's full of energy.' Eat your heart out Arsene Wenger."
Christopher Davies, Football Writers Association Book Reviews, footballwriters.co.uk

"The wonderful book *Got, Not Got* – more of the same can be found on their equally superb blog."
ThreeMatchBan.com

"It is far more enjoyable to think about football in times past, and it is a seam that is tapped so richly by authors Derek Hammond and Gary Silke, who have written a wonderful A to Z of lost football culture, treasure and pleasures."
The Blackpool Gazette

"A book exploring the lost culture of the game when pitches were mudbaths, managers wore sheepskin coats and players were too embarrassed to dive - a bygone age that seems a far cry from the profit-driven game today played in the main by overpaid primadonnas."
Paul Suart, *Birmingham Evening Mail*

"Kampprogrammer, fotballfrimarker, fotboltegneseriert… smakfullt illustrert. Just get yourself one!"
PIN magazine, Norway

"This was in WSAG's Christmas stocking and it's fantastic.
Co-written by one of our fanzine chums Gary Silke, editor of The Fox, it is an amazing collection of half-forgotten things and much loved memories. It covers mainly the 1970s when football itself seemed more innocent (probably only because we were all still at school back then).
But if you're the same age as us then this book has your name all over it.
Admiral kits, football Action Men, League Ladders, Esso badges. On and on we could go…
Buy it. Well worth it."
When Skies Are Grey

"Outstanding."
Miniboro.com, the Middlesbrough FC, art and interviews website

"A great read with fantastic visuals, the book reflects on how football used to be before the sanitisation of the Premier League. Amusing and quirky, this book captures the spirit of football from the terraces. This book is an absolute must for any footballing household."
King of the Kippax

"*Got, Not Got* is wonderful. I'm feeling quite emotional leafing through it!"
Nick Alatti, The Bridge 102.5FM in the Black Country

"In an imaginary Victorian boozer in a sepia-tinted corner of the globe, old blokes gather to talk about football back when it was good. It is a tempting retreat, with some fantastic flagship vehicles such as *Got, Not Got* and 500 Reasons To Love Football using modern media to hark back to a glorious past."
theseventytwo.com

"It would have been easy to just produce a book of nostalgic memorabilia.
It's something else to have a book that captures the heart and soul of the time.
I didn't just look back fondly, I had flashbacks full of excitement!
A wonderful journey back into our childhoods…"
God, Charlton and Punk Rock blog

"A real treat – the ideal Christmas gift for anybody who loves their retro football.
With a page dedicated to Hull City, 'Fer Ark' and all, this is the perfect football book for this time of year."
Hull City FC official website

"Whatever the football fad that accompanied the era that you got into football, you'll find it all revisited in the wonderful book *Got, Not Got*. It's a great book, every page has a throwback memory for any football fan over 30 and you'll dip in and out of it for months on end as I have done."
Nick Sports Junkie blog